CACTI
AND SUCCULENTS

KEN MARCH

COLLINS

Products mentioned in this book

Benlate* + 'Activex'	contains	benomyl
'Keriroot'	contains	NAA + captan
'Rapid'	contains	pirimicarb
'Sybol'	contains	pirimiphos-methyl

Products marked thus *'Sybol'* are trade marks of Imperial Chemical Industries plc
Benlate* is a registered trade mark of Du Pont's
Read the label before you buy: use pesticides safely..

Editors Maggie Daykin, Susanne Mitchell
Designer Chris Walker
Picture research Moira McIlroy

First published 1988 by
William Collins Sons & Co Ltd
London · Glasgow · Sydney
Auckland · Toronto · Johannesburg

© Marshall Cavendish Limited 1988

British Library Cataloguing in Publication Data

March, Ken
    Cacti and succulents. —— (Collins Aura
    garden handbooks).
    1. Succulent plants
    I. Title
    635.9'55   SB438

    ISBN 0–00–412394–8

Photoset by Bookworm Typesetting
Printed and bound in Hong Kong by Dai Nippon Printing
Company

Front cover: Echinocereus baileyi
Back cover: Cactus house
Both by Pat Brindley

CONTENTS

INTRODUCTION

Cacti and other succulents have long occupied a special place among botanists and plant collectors throughout the world. Their unusual shapes, sizes and forms, sometimes verging on the grotesque, have gained for them a particular affection among younger enthusiasts. Indeed some of the best collections of cacti and succulents were started when the owners were still school-children.

Part of the reason for this widespread interest must be due to the amazing capability of the plants to withstand extremely high temperatures and light intensities coupled with an ability to endure periods of drought. Many cacti and succulents can tolerate air temperatures of up to 50°C (120°F) approximately, although soil temperatures may rise to about 60°C (140°F) approximately due to the absorption of radiation from the sun. Coupled with this, many cacti and succulents can survive on a mere 7.5cm (3in) of rainfall per annum.

The ability to suffer such extremes makes the range of plants ideal for the forgetful enthusiast who can give space to this interesting group either on a window-sill that is in direct light or in a conservatory or greenhouse.

Where they grow The distribution of these fascinating plants is equally interesting. While succulents can be found in America, Africa and even Australia, most cacti can only be found in North and South America with just a very few exceptions such as epiphytic cacti being found in parts of Africa.

Cacti and succulents do not however live in pure desert conditions as is popularly believed. They grow in conditions of semi-desert, but always where there is some soil present, never in pure sand. Many succulents are also found in less usual places – growing close to the tops of mountains for example.

Some succulents are epiphytes and are tree-living, being found growing on trees in rain forests where their ability to grow on a small root system with a minimal

Many cacti come from North America, such as this region of Arizona. They grow in conditions of semi-desert and not in pure desert conditions as is popularly believed.

Large collections of cacti and succulents can be admired in botanic gardens, both in Britain and abroad, where they are generally planted out rather than pot grown.

reserve of water helps them to exploit their potential even in such a difficult situation.

Succulents that grow close to the tops of mountains not only tolerate high light levels, but also the extremes of temperature which can drop to around freezing point. Some varieties can even grow quite close to the snow-line on mountains and have adapted to the conditions by developing thicker, waxier tissue or producing a dense covering of wool or fine spines as protection and insulation.

When the great plant collectors of the sixteenth and seventeenth centuries accompanied explorers on their world travels, the discovery of cacti and other succulents, particularly in the New World of the Americas, caused a tremendous interest. Great collections were started in Europe and much research and study was made of the plants as they were classified and listed by such famous botanists as Linnaeus, who established the name cactus for the first time in his work classifying the plant families of the world.

Practical uses Although few cacti and succulents have any real commercial value, they have been used in several interesting ways. The fruit of the opuntia or Prickly Pear was once commercially developed to provide a major food. Although this idea for its widespread cultivation failed, it is still grown on a lesser scale for this purpose.

Some cacti have a melon-like quality, consisting as they do of over 95 per cent water. Some varieties of opuntia can be made into a conserve, while the famous alcoholic spirit tequila is made from the fleshy tissue of a variety of agave; another can be made into wine and the fibrous tissue of yet another is made into rope.

Cacti have also been used as a hedging which is not only stock-proof but likely to deter rustlers.

It is surprising the confusion that exists in defining the difference between cacti and succulents, especially when – to be botanically correct – cacti are just as much succulents as succulents are! The correct way to refer to cacti and succulents is as cacti and *other* succulents, the only real difference being that cacti are equipped with spines that emerge from areoles on the plant.

Cacti produce many types of spines, depending upon the variety of the plant. These vary from the minute, barely visible spines on certain species of opuntia or Prickly Pear to the fierce and awesome spines of the echinocactus or Barrel Cactus that can be up to approximately 7.5cm (3in) long. Although the larger spines obviously provide dramatic protection to the cactus on which they are borne, even the tiniest, almost invisible spines can be a very effective deterrent.

Anyone who has brushed against an opuntia will have quickly found that the tiny bristles lodge in the skin causing a most aggravating and irritating effect that is hard to relieve, especially as they are so difficult to see when you try to remove them. In this respect, rather than using tweezers to probe for the offending bristles, adhesive tape applied to the area will help you to pull them out with the minimum possible discomfort.

Apart from acting as a defence mechanism, spines are possibly a type of primitive leaf and they act as a life-conserving mechanism to protect the plant from extreme lack of water such as occurs during periods of excessive drought. Apart from providing some shade protection, the spines may actually help to reduce water loss as the cactus body begins to shrivel and the spines become closer together, thus increasing their protective shield effect.

Succulents, or perhaps one should say the remaining types of succulent, vary dramatically in shape and size. Although similar to cacti in that they have the facility to store water in a swollen storage organ, the development of succulents can be quite different. Whereas cacti may consist of pads, or columnar or barrel-like, swollen modified stems, other succulents vary from what may appear to be a spine-less cactus form to one that looks rather like a conventional plant, but which happens to have much fleshier leaves.

LEFT Usually, the tall or columnar cacti take many years to reach flowering size.

RIGHT Many of the smaller-growing cacti and succulents flower freely from an early age.

BELOW Opuntias have tiny bristles which lodge in the skin if you brush against them.

FAR BELOW The spines of true cacti grow from areoles.

Cacti and other succulents share the extraordinary characteristic of being able to store fluids for long periods, enabling them to survive periods of drought in their natural habitat. Apart from this ability, cacti and other succulents can also tolerate very high levels of light intensity as well as extremes of temperature.

To some people, cacti and other succulents with their characteristic swollen stems, leaves, pads and other shapes appear to be somewhat grotesque. However, many of them also produce an amazing array of flowers, from tiny insignificant ones to brilliant, gaudy blossoms that can measure up to 30cm (1ft) across.

Many of these flowers are among the most exotic and exquisite in the plant kingdom, making these unusual plants well worth collecting. Some of the most attractive flowers literally dwarf many varieties of cacti, a characteristic that applies especially to popular varieties of epiphyllum (Orchid Cactus) and echinopsis (Window-sill Cactus).

It is always harder to know how to develop a collection of cacti and other succulents than it is perhaps to start one, but with such a wealth of choice it will not be long before you realize that some degree of specialization is the best way to contain your growing interest.

LEFT Indoors, small succulents are often grown in bowls, an especially popular method with children.

RIGHT Some people collect only one group of plants, such as the mammillarias, many of which are very free-flowering. A greenhouse is recommended for a large collection.

Some collectors may identify a particular group of plants that are of special interest, such as epiphyllum, rebutia or agave for example. This interest in cultivating a specific group is often aroused by the subtle differences between the member plants. The quest for new varieties is of particular interest to such collectors as their involvement develops.

Most collections, however, eventually comprize of a very wide range of plants. This type appeals not only to the enthusiast, but also to others less committed but who will find much more of interest among the diversity of colour and form apparent in such a collection. Due to its immense range, a broadly-based collection also offers a further benefit in that there is always likely to be something of special interest to be seen as plants flower, produce side-shoots or fruit.

Things to consider Before starting the collection, it is important to decide first where it is going to be cultivated as this is fairly crucial. A window-sill collection is best comprized of spine-less succulents or smaller cacti such as rebutia or epiphytic cacti such as the schlumbergera or Christmas Cactus. Larger specimens, including cacti with larger spines, can be kept together in a greenhouse which is probably the best place to house them, although even a conservatory can serve almost as well provided that some of the more fiercely spined subjects are not included.

It is important to bear in mind that some of the more aggressive subjects such as echinocactus or Barrel Cactus are best not housed where people are easily likely to come into contact with them, otherwise a nasty injury may occur.

If a greenhouse is carefully designed to house the collection, with due consideration given to providing ventilation to avoid excess humidity, heating to avoid excessively low temperatures and effective staging (with careful placing of shelves or hanging baskets) a very wide range of plants can be housed together satisfactorily. However, take care to avoid water drips from the roof and ventilators, or from shelving and hanging baskets badly positioned above plants that may well have a lower requirement for water.

Starting the collection with a few representatives from the rebutia, mammillaria, lobivia, opuntia and possibly epiphyllum or schlumbergera families of cacti – together with succulents such as aloe, kalanchoe and the diminutive conophytum – will provide a reasonably broad base of interest for the start of a collection that will suit either a window-sill location or one that will eventually develop in the controlled environment of a greenhouse.

Avoid larger specimens or those with fierce spines or sharp ends or edges to the leaves or stems. Also avoid strong-smelling plants such as the stapelia; it may look interesting and relatively compact and may produce attractive flowers, but it has a rather nasty shock in store for occupants of the house. The smell of the stapelia (rather like rotting carrion) is nothing short of revolting and attracts flies to the flowers to pollinate them.

Unless the house has large windows that will provide full light to plants sited on a table very close by, most cacti and succulents will need to be positioned on a widow-sill. However, if a collection is to be kept in the home be sure to include one of the hoya, especially Hoya bella. This magnificent plant is ideal for a hanging pot that can be sited further into the room, away from direct sunlight, where it will produce myriad pink and white flowers in clusters that hang prettily and can best be appreciated by looking up into the clusters.

Remember also that while a greenhouse collection offers ample scope to house a very wide range of plants, a collection for the house should be carefully made to ensure that varieties give maximum interest throughout the year and make the best use of available space.

Cacti and other succulents, although relatively easy to keep, are not as one would first expect them to be in terms of self-sufficiency. For instance, many people erroneously believe that cacti and succulents require hardly any water at all throughout the year. In consequence, the plants are left in a relatively torpid state and once enthusiastic owners lose interest. Don't let that happen to you and yours.

LEFT Unlike most houseplants, cacti and succulents do not need to be repotted every year in order to grow well.

Watering The truth is that while the majority of cacti and succulents require virtually no water at all through the winter months, they do need to be watered fairly regularly through the spring and summer when they are actively growing. The dormant season lasts from around October to March and during this time almost all cacti and succulents dramatically slow down their growing processes, almost to the state of hibernation. If plants are kept even slightly moist during this period they may suffer from a stem or root rot, problems that they are particularly subject to at this time.

However, if they are kept on the dry side, it is quite surprising what cacti and succulents can tolerate. Despite the dismally low light intensities and very short length of days over the winter period some cacti and succulents can tolerate temperatures down to 4°C (40°F), although ideally they should be kept above 7°C (45°F), to avoid any likelihood of problems. Particular care should be taken when cultivating cacti and succulents in a greenhouse for, especially during the winter period, condensation or rain can drip regularly in certain places. If these are not identified early enough and the plants removed to a different location, they will almost certainly suffer premature death.

During the growing season – which is generally from March/April through to September/October – the frequency of watering can be steadily increased as the weather improves and the light level and day length increases. However, even during the height of summer take great care not to over-water. Allow the plants to almost dry out in between waterings, otherwise loss may occur from over-watering. This is a general rule as water requirements will obviously vary quite a lot between different varieties.

There is a further exception to the rule with conophytum, one of the forms of the fascinating Living Stones, Flowering Stones or even Cone Plants. These extraordinary succulents actually resemble small pebbles and grow close to the ground although not perhaps so easily thus mistaken as other types of Living Stones called lithops. As is the case with most other succulents, conophytum should be kept cooler and drier over the winter period until watering is recommenced in March/April. However, that is where the similarity ends, for in May/June the watering should be stopped and only recommenced in July/August. In September/October the plant should flower, just as it enters its next dormant period over winter.

Although the quality of the water is not as crucial as it would need to be if one was growing gardenias or other acid-loving plants, there are still guidelines to be followed.

Tap-water is usually perfectly acceptable to cacti and succulents, but it can produce certain problems, particularly when it is very cold. If cold water droplets are allowed to lay on the surface of the tissue of some plants, the effect of the temperature variance coupled with the magnifying quality of the water-droplet can result in unsightly scorch marks on the plants. Sadly, this can render the plant not worth keeping any more because of the disfigurement, particularly when the plant has a single stem rather than pads or leaves which could perhaps be removed.

Apart from water temperature, in parts of the country where chalk is present in the tap-water this, too, can cause a problem. It can result in unsightly deposits on the tissue as the water evaporates leaving the salts deposited as spots of tiny white crystals. As these are difficult to remove without causing damage to the plant, the problem may best be avoided by either watering with great care so that water droplets do not lay on the plant, or to water with clean rain-water.

If you do use rain-water, collect it in a clean container and ensure that this is cleaned out at least once or twice a year. If this is not done dead leaves and other detritus can collect and can encourage the growth of organisms such as fungal diseases which can then infect plants on to which they are applied in the water.

Use tepid water and direct it towards the compost, not the plants as they are easily spoilt by unsightly salt deposits as the water evaporates.

ABOVE AND ABOVE
RIGHT A wide range
of plants can be grown
together in a
greenhouse if it has
good ventilation, is
well heated, is not
excessively humid
and has strong,
sturdy staging.

Temperature As mentioned earlier, cacti and other succulents can tolerate a relatively wide temperature range down to around 4°C (40°F), although they are happier at a minimum of 7°C (45°F).

During spring and summer they will happily tolerate quite high temperatures and will have a higher water requirement. However, during winter try to keep them cool, around 10°C (50°F) and on the dry side with hardly any, if any, water apart from a small amount for plants showing signs of dehydration. A cool, dry winter followed by a warm, more moist spring and summer helps to stimulate flower production quite dramatically.

Feeding Cacti and succulents do occasionally need to be fed to promote healthy if not vigorous growth. However, care should be taken not to apply fertilizers at all during the dormant season over winter or in excess during the growing season.

From the end of April until early September a liquid fertilizer can be applied once every two to four weeks at a reduced rate to that recommended for pot plants. It is generally not advisable to use a houseplant fertilizer as this is usually higher in nitrogen than the other two major elements, phosphorus and potassium. Too much nitrogen can produce excessively soft and sometimes etiolated growth which, because of its softness and being too lush can be very susceptible to disease.

Ideally a tomato fertilizer such as Tomato 'Plus', used at one third to one half of the strength recommended for tomatoes, once every two to four weeks will not only help to promote stocky growth but, because of the higher potassium content, may stimulate flower production.

Whenever a plant is fed with a liquid fertilizer it is worth first checking to ensure that the plant is not completely dry at the roots, otherwise damage may be caused by the fertilizer solution. Plants should be barely moist or if dry should be lightly moistened with water prior to being fed.

Apart from liquid fertilizers, slow release fertilizers or organic fertilizers such as bone-meal may be used. This can be just as effective; the nutrient requirement of cacti and succulents is quite low and suited to a prolonged release formula.

Light The great majority of cacti and other succulents prefer to be grown in a well lit situation and for this reason are probably most happy when grown in a greenhouse or conservatory. Plants grown indoors on a window-sill, even in what we would consider full light, are never likely to be exposed to the same level of light and as such can often produce growth which is quite out of character for the plant in question. Symptoms of this may be etiolation of the stem or what can only be described as an 'expanded' appearance on plants such as mammillaria.

However, unless you are a perfectionist you can still grow many cacti and succulents to a quite acceptable standard on a well lit, preferably south-facing window-sill.

Surprisingly, even though most cacti and succulents enjoy high light levels, scorch damage can sometimes occur when the sun's rays are magnified through the glass. The most likely time for this to happen is in the early spring when the plant's tissue is most susceptible to damage. This is because it tends to become more delicate during the winter and therefore less resistant to damage in the early spring sunshine.

ABOVE Dish gardens of succulents, used as home decoration, can if desired be stood out of doors for the summer.

RIGHT The Christmas cactus is an ideal subject for a hanging container.

As a rule, pot tall plants in a container that has a diameter equal to half the length of the plant (not counting roots). Rounded succulents should fit the pot quite snuggly, with just 2.5cm (1in) to spare.

There are also a number of cacti and succulents that prefer to be grown out of prolonged direct sunshine. Plants such as hoya and epiphyllum, which often grow as epiphytes in rain forests, are happy to be grown further into the room, away from direct sunlight.

Another effect of light is caused by the length of daylight hours. Some varieties of succulent, such as kalanchoe, are sensitive to day length to determine their time of flowering. Perhaps surprisingly it requires more hours of darkness than daylight to successfully initiate flowering.

Re-potting Unlike houseplants, cacti and succulents do not need to be re-potted every year or so to get the best out of them. However, it is quite wrong to think that they can or should be left in the same pot of compost for ever.

Cacti and succulents prefer to be grown in a pot only moderately larger in dimensions than the plant;

over-potting makes them more susceptible to being over-watered.

Although the more vigorous growing varieties can be potted into larger pots, it is more usual to re-pot plants back into the same pots in which they were growing but in fresh compost.

Whatever the reason for re-potting, never do so during the dormant season of October to March as this can render the plant susceptible to various problems, from root damage to stem or root rots. The best time to re-pot is from April to September, especially during the earlier months when they can quickly establish and settle into the new compost.

If possible, use clay pots as these are without doubt the best for cacti and succulents. Being porous they allow air to permeate and water to evaporate more freely, providing a more acceptable environment for the plant. Plastic pots often encourage an airless condition in the pot which in turn can lead to root problems.

RIGHT A folded paper 'collar' is a useful means of handling spiny plants when they are being repotted.

A very free-draining compost consisting of equal parts of loam, peat and a sharp grade of sand or grit is the most traditional compost for cacti although this can be varied to suit, provided the mixture is always free draining. Alternatively, a specially formulated proprietary cactus compost can be used.

Prickly plants are best handled with thick leather gardening gloves or by wrapping the plant in a 'bandage' of folded newspaper.

If potting the plant back into the same pot, a dessertspoon or small trowel can be useful to infill with compost around the plant. Alternatively, if potting into a larger pot, use the earlier, smaller pot to create a depression of the correct size in the centre of the new pot of compost to take the plant's root-ball. Then place the plant in the depression and gently firm in. Then leave the plant for three or four days before watering, as this will help the plant to adapt better.

Training Although the majority of cacti and succulents do not require training, there are some that will benefit from such attention.

Some of the taller, more vigorous forms of cacti that produce strong, erect columns look quite magnificent and whenever possible should be left to be self-supporting. However, they and a few of the more irregularly-growing cacti such as opuntia may need the support of a carefully placed stake.

Epiphyllum and especially selenicereus may sometimes become rather lanky, in which case they, too, need support to train the plant to best effect.

When using stakes, choose one that is not too obtrusive. Also, do not use narrow wire or string that may cut into the tissue of the plant and cause damage.

Rather than resorting to the use of artificial support you could trim any wayward parts of the plant, using a sharp knife. Plants such as hoya can also be trimmed back to promote a more balanced and compact growth.

A further method of training a plant can be employed when growing tall specimens in a greenhouse. Rather than staking and tying the plant, the subject can be tied somewhere near the tip and the line tied to one of the roof members.

PESTS AND DISEASES

Despite the fact that cacti and other succulents have generally tougher tissue than most other plants, they are still at risk from the ravages of pests and diseases. Although the incidence of an infestation or infection is somewhat less, it is important to inspect the plants regularly for early signs so that appropriate action can be taken before any serious damage can result in the plant's disfigurement or death.

PESTS

Aphids The aphid family consists of a wide range of insects with long pointed mouthparts that are used to stab the soft tissue of young growth. Aphids, commonly known as greenfly or blackfly, are particularly active during the spring and summer and can be a problem on the flowers of cacti and succulents.

Fortunately, they are relatively easy to control and little damage will result from an infestation that is caught in the very early stages before the aphids can multiply. Aphids have a remarkably efficient reproductive system and their numbers can grow extremely quickly.

As soon as they are first seen spray with 'Rapid', as a liquid spray or aerosol, taking care to give the plant a satisfactory coverage – especially as aphids may also be found inside the flowers and even the flower buds.

To ensure complete control spray again seven to ten days later and then check regularly for any further signs of the pests.

Mealy Bugs These are a real nuisance and are probably the biggest pest of cacti and succulents. They look like small wood-lice, covered in a floury coating. The coating is a type of wax which helps to protect the insect, making it rather difficult to bring the infestation under control with some spray chemicals.

Although the adult insect may be

Mealy bugs are fond of cacti.

seen occasionally, the most usual sign of infestation is what look like white patches of cotton wool. These are generally found in crevices on the plant or, if it has branched leaves, between the leaf stalk and the stem.

In the early stages the damage caused by mealy bugs is relatively small but the pest should never be ignored for as its population grows the damage becomes more severe and the pest becomes extremely difficult to control.

An isolated attack can be reasonably controlled by using either a small, artists' brush dipped in methylated spirits or a matchstick with cotton wool wound around one end and soaked in the spirits. This should be applied to any adults that are found as well as to the patches of 'wool' for the young are incubated there. Failure to treat this will result in poor control.

'Sybol', used every seven to ten days for a month, should control the pest but if the 'wool' is still in evidence, continue the treatment until the plant is free. 'Sybol' can be applied as either a liquid spray or as an aerosol.

Root Mealy Bugs Unlike many other pests that can be seen relatively easily, root mealy bugs are a real nuisance because they remain hidden in the soil, feeding on the roots of the plants.

As their population increases they can seriously affect the growth rate of the plant, reducing its vigour and making it more susceptible to disease – particularly soil-borne root diseases.

Even if the pests are not found by inspection, the plant may look rather tired and lacking in life and vigour. However, it is best not to wait for these symptoms to appear; much can be gained from inspection of the plants' roots at one to two month intervals.

Root mealy bugs affect growth.

Carefully remove the plant from its pot and inspect for signs of the pest which is similar to the ordinary mealy bug, with white patches being visible on the roots. If a plant is difficult to remove from its pot and root mealy bugs are found on other plants in the collection it may be wise to treat all those suspected of suffering from the pest.

Watering the compost or dipping the plant in a solution of 'Sybol', diluted at the rate for spraying, once every ten to fourteen days for four to six weeks during the growing season is usually sufficient treatment to bring the pest under control.

Red Spider Mites These are incredibly tiny members of the spider family. However, as parasitic mites they should be controlled as soon as they are found.

Despite their name, red spider mites are actually straw coloured and almost invisible to the naked eye. Unlike many other pests they are also remarkably mobile and move about at great speed. They thrive in warm, dry conditions and have chewing mouthparts that can leave the tissue of plants discoloured and disfigured.

Apart from checking the plants regularly with a hand lens for signs of the mites, keep a close watch for any fine strands of webbing. Red spider mites use webbing to transport themselves all over the plant and to other plants and this tends to be a sign of a more advanced attack.

Spray regularly with 'Sybol' as a liquid spray or aerosol every seven to ten days for four to six weeks during the growing season to be sure of effecting control of the pest. It is particularly important to persevere with the spray treatment as the pest has a relatively long life cycle and further sprays are needed to catch the young as they hatch. Also, be sure to spray effectively to cover all of the plant with the spray solution.

Scale Insects are very good at camouflaging themselves. Looking like tiny blisters or regular-shaped spots or blemishes on the plant, they can remain undetected for a considerable time. This leaves them free to build up their population and cause damage as well as covering the plant with honeydew and sooty mould.

The scale insect, as its name suggests, has a small scale under which it hides, like a tortoise in its shell! The insect does not move far; as soon as it hatches under the mother's scale it moves off just a short distance to find its own feeding place and then settles down to feed off the defenceless plant.

Although mature scales can be gently scraped off with a stiff paintbrush or a fingernail, complete control will require some form of chemical treatment.

Control of the pest can best be achieved by spraying every seven to ten days for four to six weeks to catch the young as they hatch, using either the liquid spray or aerosol formulation of 'Sybol'.

DISEASES
Fungal rots Probably one of the biggest problems suffered by cacti and succulents is that of fungal rots. These can take the form of root rots which can dramatically affect a plant in a very short period of time, or of fungal spots or lesions small as a pin-head or large enough to rot a large part of the plant or stem.

Although a fungal organism is responsible for the parasitic damage to the plant, fungal problems quite often occur when the plant has been stressed, such as when too wet at the roots or being grown in a cool, damp position, or scorched.

To try to avoid fungal problems occurring, at all times take care in the plant's cultivation, to ensure that it is not subjected to traumas. However, chemical treatments such as Benlate + 'Activex' for spraying or dipping may be useful.

Where root loss has occurred remove the decaying roots and drench the compost with Benlate + 'Activex'. Then pot the plant in either a 50/50 mix of a sand and cactus compost or even pure sand and keep the plant at 20°C (68°F) or above until it has produced healthy new roots.

Caution Always be sure to follow the manufacturers' recommendations and instructions before using any chemical, taking particular care regarding children, pets and wildlife. It is imperative to follow their safety measures and to pay careful attention to notes regarding the susceptibility of certain plants to be damaged by the chemical.

Kalanchoes and crassulas, for example, are particularly susceptible to some chemical sprays, so always check before treating your plants, otherwise you could cause more damage than the pest would have done if left unchecked.

Always spray on a calm day. Be sure to spray thoroughly but lightly and do not over-dose; always use the chemical at the recommended rate and do not increase this amount.

It is also a wise precaution not to spray in direct sunlight or on flowers as scorch may occur. If the plant is large enough and you are doubtful about whether it may be damaged, first apply a small amount of the spray to a discreet area and inspect carefully for any signs of damage after seven to fourteen days.

PROPAGATION

Much fun can be gained from propagating cacti and other succulents from seed, cuttings, or even grafting. The techniques described below are quite straightforward and are worth attempting, especially as when they are successful your collection will increase at a minimal cost and a real sense of achievement and satisfaction can be gained.

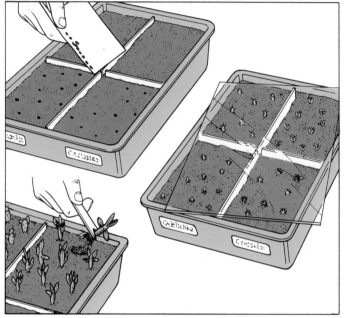

Use a seed box for seed-sowing and a proprietary cactus compost. Sow thinly and lightly cover with fine sand.
Cover box with a sheet of glass and place in warm conditions.
When the seedlings are large enough to handle, prick them out into individual pots.

Seed Despite the fact that cacti and other succulents may not always come true from seed (especially in the case of certain varieties of cacti) germinating them from seed is very interesting and rewarding and does not take as long as you might think.

In preparation, try to obtain fresh seed to ensure the best possible germination rate. This may either be collected from your own flowering plants or obtained from a specialist seed supplier.

If the seed is collected directly from flowering plants, allow the seed to mature and dry in the seed pod before sowing. Once separated from the pod or dry husk the seed can be placed in a small paper envelope until you are ready to sow the seed. Remember to write the name of the plant on the envelope – and if taking seeds from several varieties, place them in separate packets.

Select a suitable shallow container such as a half pot or pan, or even a small seed tray and lightly fill to within about 1cm (½in) of the top, using a proprietary cactus compost. To improve drainage and ease of pricking-out the seedlings, sharp sand may be added to the compost (approximately 10–20 per cent by volume).

The compost should be just moist, but not too wet prior to sowing the seed, which may either be lightly sown directly on to the surface of the compost or pre-mixed with a small quantity of fine sand to bulk up the seed and ease the sowing process. A small quantity of fine sand may be applied over the seed as a very light covering, although this is by no means essential.

Then cover the seed with glass and keep it out of direct sunlight, at a temperature of about 21°C (70°F), until germination has taken place; this may be anything from three or four days to a month or so. As soon as the seed has germinated, water lightly as necessary with either a light mist of water or by partially immersing the container, not quite to the level of the compost surface.

Seed is best sown in March if bottom heat can be provided, otherwise it is better to wait until the weather and ambient temperature improves in May, or a little later, depending on the supply of seed. Do not sow too late in the season, otherwise the tiny seedlings may not be strong enough to survive the sometimes extreme cold of winter.

As soon as the seed has germinated remove the glass cover and allow the seedlings to develop. When they are large enough to handle, gently prick them out and pot them up in a proprietary cactus compost. The size obviously will vary according to the variety and your own capability to handle them effectively, but generally about 13mm (½in) should be a good size at which to undertake pricking-out.

ABOVE A seed capsule of *Gymnocalycium glaucum*.

LEFT A newly germinated cactus seed. Germination may take anything from a few days to several weeks.

ABOVE RIGHT Seedlings should be potted into individual pots as soon as they are large enough to handle easily.

BELOW Lithops or living stones seedlings at about the right size for pricking out or potting.

materials such as compost, containers and so on are sterile, to minimize the risk of disease and to increase the success rate.

Cuttings The variation of shape and form of cacti and other succulents offers almost endless possibilities for many plants to be propagated by cuttings. Whereas plants raised from seed may not come true to variety, cuttings will get over that problem, although the potential for increasing stock will not be as dramatic.

Cuttings may be taken from leaf-pads, off-shoots or even by division as cacti and succulents produce small plantlets.

The best time to take cuttings is during spring and summer or even early autumn, although beware of the onset of poor weather and reduced ambient temperatures late in the season.

If the seed takes a relatively long time to germinate the growth of algae on the surface of the compost may become a problem. If this is the case a solution of copper sulphate lightly sprayed on to the surface may help and also reduce the further likelihood of damping-off occurring.

Finally, it is very important that when dealing with young and potentially delicate plants, care is taken at every stage to ensure that all

Prior to taking any cuttings select a sharp knife or scalpel and ensure that it is clean and sterile; pass the

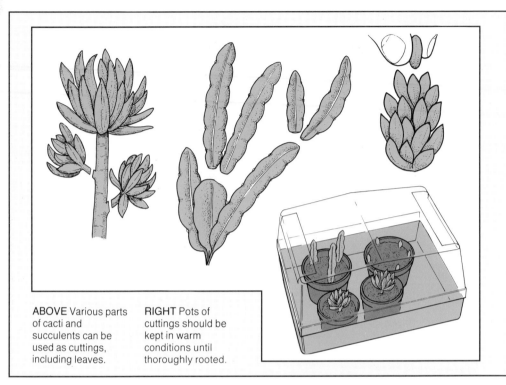

ABOVE Various parts of cacti and succulents can be used as cuttings, including leaves.

RIGHT Pots of cuttings should be kept in warm conditions until thoroughly rooted.

blade through a flame to kill any bacteria or fungi if you are taking a number of cuttings, to help reduce the possible transfer of pathogens.

The cuttings should then be carefully removed, making a clean cut to avoid damage to the parent plant. If necessary, the cuttings should then be trimmed to provide the best surface for rooting. They should then be left to callous. This may take only a couple of days or so for many succulents, small cuttings or epiphytic cacti, or as long as one to two weeks for the fleshier, bulkier cacti. While being left to callous the cuttings should be kept out of direct sunlight to prevent dehydration.

The calloused cuttings should be dipped in 'Keriroot' hormone rooting powder to improve rooting and help to reduce rotting off ('Keriroot' includes captan as a fungicide). Dip only about 13mm (½in) of the base of the cutting in 'Keriroot', then insert it in either a peat/sand mix or a similar material to that used for the germination of cacti and succulents seed, using the higher sand content media.

Gently insert the cutting into the compost; do not compact the compost or insert the cutting too deeply, otherwise rotting may occur. If necessary, support any unstable cuttings with stakes or similar means until rooting has taken place.

Maintain a temperature of about 21°C (70°F) until the cuttings have rooted satisfactorily before potting up as required.

Grafting Grafting is a specialized process to propagate either the unusual or sometimes extraordinary varieties; for example, the bright

Grafting – the scion should be held securely on the stock until they unite.

The cut areas of the scion and stock must be of the same size for successful grafting.

yellow or pink chlorophyll-free plants from Japan which could not grow unless grafted.

Plants such as rhipsalis and zygocactus which are naturally hanging or trailing epiphytic cacti can be grafted on to pereskia to produce a standard effect not unlike that of a standard fuchsia. Other plants such as opuntia, pereskiopsis, trichocereus as well as pereskia may be used as plants to graft on to.

Succulents should however be grafted on to the same family to 'take' effectively.

Use a clean, sharp knife or scalpel to prepare the 'stock' (base part) by making a slanting cut upwards to the area where the graft will be placed. This helps to avoid the problem of excess moisture collecting and rotting off being encouraged.

The 'scion' (top part) should be similarly prepared so that the cut areas are of the same size although no slanting cut is required. The top (scion) should then be placed on or inserted in the bottom piece (stock) and held in place by either tooth picks, cactus spines or rigid nylon bristles. If necessary, a piece of netting such as that used as packing for oranges may be placed over the scion and weighted with a few coins to keep it in place. The graft should be covered with a polythene bag or clear plastic cover (ensuring that it does not touch the plant) to encourage a more rapid union and kept at about 21°C (70°F) for up to two months.

After about a month the support materials may be carefully removed.

After the second month the union should be secure and the carefully nurtured plant can be grown on.

SIXTY OF THE BEST

One of the delights of growing cacti and succulents is the enormous variety of species from which to build up a personal collection – but to the new enthusiast this wealth of choice can be too much of a good thing! So, to set you on the right tracks, here is a selection of sixty plants of particular merit, and all easy to grow.

Agave americana 'Marginata'

The agaves, sometimes commonly called Century Plants, are fairly demanding as far as space is concerned. One of the most popular is the *A. americana* 'Marginata' or Variegated Century Plant.

It is not however the type of plant to have if there are small children around as the variegated, cream edged, green, strap-like leaves end in a sharp-pointed spike and have equally sharp, barb-like protrusions along the length of the leaf.

The very durable and tough leaves are formed in a rosette which can grow up to approximately 75cm (2½ft), and when the spike of greenish-yellow flowers appears, may grow to over 2m (6 ½ft) in height.

A more manageable species is the Queen Victoria Century Plant, *A. victoriae-reginae*, which has no barbs on the green leaves and is smaller in stature and more compact at about 30cm (1ft) with a greenish flowered spike up to around 2m (6½ft) or more. Once the Agave has flowered the rosette dies, although further off-shoots are produced by the plant.

Agaves will happily tolerate a summer season outside and, indeed, can be grown outdoors provided they are not exposed to frost.

Aloe aristata

A compact species sometimes called the Lace Aloe, which will happily tolerate a little light shade. The compact, fleshy rosette form of the plant measures approximately 15cm (6in) across and consists of dark green leaves with white flecks standing slightly proud of the leaf surface.

The plant freely produces rosettes which should be separated regularly to avoid overcrowding.

Growing to approximately 20cm (8in) in height, *A. aristata* will produce flower spikes of relatively uninteresting, yellowish flowers, up to 45cm (1½ft) high.

Agave americana 'Marginata'.

Aloe aristata, the lace aloe.

Aloe variegata **is popular.**

Aloe variegata

Known as the Partridge-Breasted Aloe, this is a very attractive and commonly cultivated form of aloe with broad, fleshy, green leaves with bold, silvery-white stripes. It makes an excellent houseplant, growing to about 30cm (1ft) in height, and produces reddish-coloured tubular flowers on a spike up to 30cm (1ft) in height.

As the plant grows the weight of the rosette will be quite surprising and care should be taken to ensure that it does not become top-heavy, otherwise a topple can result in the beautiful bold leaves becoming damaged and disfiguring the plant.

The *A. variegata* is again happy grown out of direct sunlight, in partial light shade. However, it can easily be over-watered causing loss of some roots and leaves or even the whole plant. On the other hand, an excessively dry plant will very quickly start to look dishevelled.

Aporocactus flagelliformis

This rather lazily trailing cactus of ribbed, cylindrical stems is commonly called the Rat's Tail Cactus. Apart from being a good window-sill cactus, it is also very effective in a hanging basket or, for a more dramatic effect, may be grafted on to a columnar stock to provide a standard appearance.

The long stems are covered with brownish spines and the plant produces attractive red or pink flowers, depending on the cultivar. Although relatively short-lived (only up to about four days), these flowers are extremely attractive. In time the stems grow too long and need to be cut off, allowing sufficient room for the smaller stems to take over. The pieces that have been removed may be propagated if required.

Aporocactus flagelliformis.

Astrophytum myriostigma

This extraordinary cactus, with broad ribs on a cylinder-shaped plant, is commonly called the Bishop's Cap or, sometimes, Bishop's Mitre. Although it has no spines, the brownish areoles are still present and are quite a feature against the green body of the plant.

Grown in the greenhouse or as a houseplant it will reach about 15–20cm (6–8in) in height, producing extremely attractive flowers that contrast with the somewhat ordinary appearance of the plant. The yellow flowers, which are about 5cm (2in) in diameter, often appear in succession.

Carnegiea gigantea

Probably grown as much for its novelty value as anything else, the *C. gigantea* or saguaro in time will grow into the typical branched cactus seen in many Western films. Although very slow growing, it can eventually reach 15–18m (50–60ft) in height and 60cm (2ft) in breadth in its natural habitat, but is more likely to be seen up to 30cm (1ft) in the home or greenhouse.

Cephalocereus senilis.

Astrophytum myriostigma.

The white, trumpet-shaped flowers are most unlikely to be produced on cultivated plants; usually being seen only on wild specimens aged between 50 and 200 years. The characteristic branches are produced as the plant nears middle-age.

Cephalocereus senilis

This rather strange but attractive cactus has an appeal all of its own. It is long-lived – up to 200 years in the wild – slow growing and covered with brownish-yellow spines on a ribbed green stem.

The usually white or pink flowers are very short-lived – lasting only one night – and are not produced until the plant approaches middle-age. The appeal of the plant is the tangle of white woolly hair that it grows in a straggly habit, especially on its top, inspiring the common name of Old Man Cactus.

The plant may reach 12–15m (40–50ft) in height at 200 years but it very rarely grows to more than 30cm (1ft) in the home.

Chamaecereus silvestrii

Often beloved by school-children as one of the first cacti in their collection, the Peanut Cactus is easy to grow. Its spine-covered cylindrical stems grow horizontally up to 15cm (6in) in length but quite often do not stay attached to the parent plant for long enough to reach this size. However, those that do come adrift are good subjects for propagation, rooting readily.

Chamaecereus produces bright red flowers, up to 5cm (2in) in length, provided the plant is grown in full sunlight.

Conophytum bilobum

This unusual succulent only grows up to 19mm (¾in) tall and consists of pairs of fleshy, succulent green leaves that are joined together and from which emerge bright yellow, daisy-like flowers.

Echeveria setosa **is downy.**

The plant likes good light and although diminutive in size, as it spreads to fill the pot it is quite attractive, especially if it is offset by a light covering of shingle sprinkled on to the surface of the compost.

Care is required to avoid over-watering, with some modification of the normal care in that after the normal treatment over winter and in the spring, watering should be stopped in May/June until July/August when watering should be recommenced. Flowering is likely to occur in September/October.

Crassula falcata

This extraordinary succulent has bold, fleshy, silvery grey-green leaves growing to about 25–30cm (10–12in). Sometimes called the Scarlet Paint Brush Plant, it will produce a magnificent and quite extraordinary flower spike.

The fleshy flower stem carries a mass of extremely attractive, bright red flowers that make the plant a worthwhile and unusual addition to any collection. However, as the plant ages it tends to become rather untidy and should be propagated in order to start a new, more compact plant as a replacement.

Echeveria setosa

Echeverias are very popular succulents, forming compact rosettes. *E. setosa* is one of the most attractive, the compact green leaves having a white down-like covering of hairs.

Although diminutive in height, the plant may grow to 10–15cm (4–6in) in diameter and will produce red and yellow cup-shaped flowers on a tall flower spike.

E. setosa may be grown outside in the late spring and summer but should be brought into the greenhouse or house in September. Take particular care not to allow water to rest at the base of the rosette, otherwise rotting may occur.

Echinocactus grusonii

The magnificent Golden Barrel Cactus or Barrel Cactus improves with age, developing into a bold plant with fiercesome golden spines up to 7.5cm (3in) long on mature plants. However, it is slow growing and may take up to a hundred years to reach a diameter of 1m (3½ft) approximately.

The plant has a very high light requirement and will only produce its small yellow flowers when exposed to higher light intensities than is likely in this country, and only then on mature plants. Despite this it is worthy of being grown for the colourful golden-yellow spines on the green body of the plant.

Echinocereus engelmannii

Echinocereus are relatively small cacti but well worth collecting for their colourful and often magnificent flowers, produced even when the plants are still relatively small.

E. engelmannii is roughly columnar and grows to 20–25cm (8–10in) high, with a diameter of 4–5cm (1½-2in) approximately. The quite long spines are cream or white. As the plant grows it will produce offshoots and reddish-purple flowers to about 6.5cm (2 ½in) across.

Echinopsis eyriesii

Although the flowers of echinopsis are quite short-lived, fading after only a few days, they are certainly not to be missed. The beautiful, funnel-shaped flowers are quite splendid, making the plant one of the most popular for cultivating in the home. In fact, in Europe echinopsis are often referred to as the window-sill cactus.

E. eyriesii is probably one of the most common, with amazing large white flowers produced on relatively long stems above the plants. Echinopsis are easy to grow indoors and tolerate low winter temperatures well, provided that they are kept on the dry side at this time.

Echinopsis multiplex

E. multiplex is sometimes called the Easter Lily Cactus, which can be confusing as several other types share the same common name. Growing to about 20–25cm (8–10in) *E. multiplex* produces beautiful pink flowers that almost dwarf the plant and have a scent similar to that of the Lily.

The plant produces offsets quite readily and these can overcrowd the plant; they should therefore be removed and potted up singly. Failure to do this will result in the parent plant taking longer to reach a flowering size, and with possibly disappointing results.

Echinopsis multiplex.

32

Epiphyllum ackermannii

More commonly known as the Orchid Cactus, the epiphyllum is a beautiful epiphyte or tree-living cactus that, although rather uninteresting when not in flower, has blooms that more than compensate.

The Orchid Cactus likes a soil with a higher humus content and produces tall, flattish stems which may be either two- or three-sided; they can be rather untidy and may need support. Many varieties produce flowers of a wide colour range including yellow, orange, pink, red, lilac and white and up to 30cm (1ft) across. *E. ackermannii* produces smaller, red flowers up to 15cm (6in) across. Epiphyllums prefer not to be exposed to direct sunlight for too long; a little light shade will prevent scorching of the plant.

A variety of epiphyllum.

Espostoa lanata

Sometimes called Peruvian Old-man Cactus, this plant has a green stem covered with fine white spines and bristles similar to hair. Although the hairs are quite soft to the touch when the plant is young, they can become more coarse and wiry as it gets older, which may also diminish the plant's appeal.

Although the plant rarely flowers in cultivation, partly due to the high light requirement, it nevertheless offers a bold columnar form to complement other types being grown. However, if the collection consists mainly of smaller types, beware as the Espostoa will outgrow the others in a few years and look out of place.

***Euphorbia milii* var. *splendens*.**

Euphorbia milii var. splendens

This most unusual plant, commonly called the Crown of Thorns, looks more like a small shrub than a succulent. The woody stems produce quite vicious spines as well as green leaves which grow towards the top of the plant for part of the year.

The rose-red 'flowers' which fade in time to pink, are actually coloured bracts or modified leaves. A yellow variety is also available but this tends to grow more slowly and is not as popular.

Originating from Madagascar, the Crown of Thorns likes plenty of sunlight and can grow rather tall and straggly. Pruning back to keep the plant compact is worthwhile but should be done with care for the sap, like that of most other types of euphorbia, is poisonous.

Faucaria tigrina

Popular with school-aged collectors the *F. tigrina* is a relatively small succulent with the bold common name of Tiger's Jaws. The greenish-grey succulent, fleshy leaves are produced in pairs with 'teeth' along the edges that give the plant a fierce look, even though it is in fact quite inoffensive.

As the plant grows it tends to fill the pot with a rather untidy collection of tiny 'jaws' covering the surface. The plant also produces daisy-like yellow flowers from the centre and these close at night.

Although the plant may grow to only 10–13cm (4–5in) the flowers reach 5cm (2in) in diameter.

Ferocactus acanthodes

Ferocactus are really only for the avid collector, for these plants produce extremely fierce spines. Although this cactus may only grow to about 10–15cm (4–6in) when mature in a collection, the curved and very sharp spines may reach almost 5cm (2in) in length. However, they do make the ball-shaped plant look unusually appealing as they are tinged with red and completely cover it. In the wild this cactus grows much larger and flowers – which it very rarely does in a collection.

Ferocactus latispinus

This is possibly the best ferocactus to grow, especially if you value flowers. Although most ferocactus do not flower easily when kept in a pot, this particular one will, albeit rather late in the season.

The flowers range from violet to pink or red and appear late in the autumn but need prolonged warmth and sunshine which, if absent because of a poor autumn or early winter, may result in the abortion of the flower buds.

As with other ferocactus, take particular care with watering; despite their tough appearance they are very prone to loss through being over-watered, so beware.

Faucaria tigrina, tiger's jaws.

Ferocactus latispinus.

Gymnocalycium andreae.

Fenestraria rhopalophylla.

Fenestraria rhopalophylla

This quite extraordinary little succulent produces tiny, fleshy, whitish-green leaves in clumps measuring only about 2.5cm (1in) in height. Commonly called Babies' Toes or, more aptly, the Window Plant: the tops of the leaves feature a transparent window that allows light to reach the green pigment, chlorophyll, which produces plant foods. This adaptation developed to enable the plant to grow in harsh, near desert conditions where most of the leaves are submerged in sandy soil. In pot cultivation however, the plant normally carries the leaves above soil and these should not be buried; otherwise, rotting may occur due to the cooler conditions and lower light intensities. The Window Plant also produces pretty, white daisy-like flowers measuring up to 2.5cm (1in) across.

Gymnocalycium andreae

A greyish-green plant of quite diminutive proportions that nevertheless is everything a good cactus should be in terms of appearance and how well it flowers. Sometimes commonly called the Chin Cactus, most gymnocalycium flower well. *G. andreae* produces yellow flowers measuring approximately 2.5cm (1in) across and these tend to dwarf the plant which grows to a sphere measuring only approximately 5cm (2in) across.

G. andreae also produces offsets which may be left to enhance the parent plant, or carefully separated and propagated.

Gymnocalycium denudatum

This deep green gymnocalycium is probably the most common one grown. It produces attractive pink or white flowers in spring or summer and these measure up to 7.5cm (3in) in diameter. Although white flowers tend to be the most common, the pink form is very attractive.

This plant has acquired its common name, the Spider Cactus, from the appearance of the spines that do indeed, with a little imagination, resemble small spiders. Although larger than *G. andreae*, *G. denudatum* may still only grow to about 15cm (6in) in height.

Gymnocalycium mihanovichii
'Hibotan'

Grown normally, the attractive *G. mihanovichii* or Plaid Cactus produces yellow flowers on a greyish-green plant. However, this variety – which is one of a number of weird forms – has been artificially produced. Originally cultivated in Japan it contains little if any chlorophyll, the essential green pigment in plants. Instead, an extraordinary pinkish-red hue is present, giving the plant its common name of the Ruby Ball Cactus.

To obtain necessary nutrients the plant is grafted on to a normal cactus stock, most usually, this would be *Hylocereus* spp. Although it is not very likely, the gymnocalycium may flower, producing the normal white flowers.

Hamatocactus setispinus
Although one of the smallest cacti, measuring only 10–13cm (4–5in) in diameter when fully grown, this is a good plant for growing in the home. There are believed to be only three species of *Hamatocactus* and *H. setispinus* is probably the most common one in cultivation. One of the features of the plant is that it has beautiful, yellow, trumpet-like flowers from its tip, even when quite small. It also has deep ribs which enhance its appearance as well as long, white, quite sharp spines.

Haworthia margaritifera
Haworthias are quite happy to grow out of direct sunlight and in fairly light shade. Although the small white flowers produced on a tall stem are not spectacular they nevertheless increase the interest of the plant. *H. margaritifera* grows in a rosette form with unusual spotted leaves, to a height of approximately 15cm (6in).

Typical of all haworthias, the plant can be propagated from offsets or leaf cuttings, which are the most usual techniques, or from seed.

Hamatocactus setispinus.

Gymnocalycium mihanovichii.

Hoya bella

Surprisingly, hoya are quite often not considered to be succulents; yet no collection should be without this magnificent little plant. Growing in the wild as an epiphyte, or tree-living plant, *H. bella* is happy to be in light shade and makes a superb plant for a hanging basket.

The small, spear-shaped, dark green leaves are produced in pairs and growth is quite vigorous, requiring occasional trimming to keep a well-balanced habit. The dainty white flowers with pink centres are produced freely, often twice a year. They cascade in clusters all around the plant. Grow this succulent in a hanging basket so that you can appreciate the beauty of the flowers fully by looking up into them.

Take particular care during flowering to avoid any shock to the plant, such as extremes of temperature or overwatering which can cause the plant to abort its flowers.

Hoya bella flowers freely.

Kalanchoe daigremontiana.

Kalanchoe blossfeldiana

This grows to about 30cm (1ft) with green, fleshy, slightly serrated leaves that are roughly heart-shaped. Although the foliage is not spectacular, the very brightly coloured flowers are freely produced, smothering the foliage with vivid red, orange or yellow. Very popular as a houseplant and most often sold as a flowering houseplant, especially during the winter, it is particularly popular at Christmas.

It is easy to forget that the plant is a succulent as far as watering is concerned, which may result in the plant rotting, so due care must be exercised.

Kalanchoe daigremontiana

Although this plant is still called *Bryophyllum daigremontiana* by some, it is more correctly classified as a kalanchoe. Also called the Devil's Backbone, it can grow to be rather untidy and straggly, but is worth cultivating for its novelty value.

In time it may grow up to 75cm (2½ft), but may well require some support by staking well before then. The green leaves with a blotched pattern are quite large, measuring up to 15–20cm (6–8in).

The plant is unusual in that it produces tiny plantlets on the edges of the leaves which – complete with roots – drop off with ease when they are ready and then start to grow wherever they happen to fall.

Kleinia stapeliiformis

Similar to *K. rowleyanus*, this kleinia is also sometimes called *Senecio stapeliiformis*. The common name of Candle Plant is apt because of the unusual green stems which are up to 25cm (10in) in height although the diameter may only be 13mm (½in).

The Candle Plant produces quite extraordinary, red flowers in clusters measuring 2.5–4cm (1–1½in) in diameter on 12.5cm (5in) stems.

Lithops helmutii

Lithops are quite extraordinary little succulents and real sun-lovers. Measuring only about 1–4cm (½-1½in) in height they are close-growing and very compact. The common name of Living Stones is quite apt as they can quite easily be mistaken for pebbles, camouflaging themselves as they do among stones to avoid being eaten by animals.

Similar to the fenestraria, the Living Stone has a transparent or translucent top which allows light into the plant when the fleshy leaves are almost buried. *L. helmutii* is grey-green and produces daisy-like, bright yellow flowers measuring 2.5cm (1in) across.

Lobivia backebergii

Lobivia are very popular cacti, worthy of being in any collection for their spectacular flowers. Many of the species originate from Bolivia in South America.

L. backebergii is initially round, growing slightly more elongated with age, eventually reaching about 10cm (4in) in height and almost 5cm (2in) in width amid sharp, curved spines which are best avoided.

Lobivia hertrichiana

Although slightly larger in diameter than *L. backebergii*, measuring be-

Lithops or Living Stones.

Lobivia backebergii.

tween 7.5–10cm (3–4in) across, *L. hertrichiana* is still a relatively small plant, somewhat rounded in shape and covered with buff-coloured spines. During spring and summer it produces vivid red flowers which can measure up to 5cm (2in) in diameter.

As the plant grows it readily produces offsets which, provided they do not over-crowd the pot, make a fantastic display – covering the pot with a profusion of flowers.

Mammillaria bocasana

Mammillaria are named after the teat or nipple-like tubercles. Mammillaria are extremely popular cacti and *M. bocasana*, sometimes called the Powder-puff Cactus because of the appearance of the spines and white silky hair, is a compact plant.

The small but attractive white flowers are produced around the top of the plant rather like a halo. The spines may look quite inoffensive, but they have small hooks which have the capacity to catch on to almost anything and can be difficult to remove from the skin.

Mammillaria bocasana.

Mammillaria hahniana

This is one of the most attractive mammillarias, sometimes called the Old Lady Cactus, and sports a great deal more white hair than the Powder-puff Cactus, *M. bocasana*.

As the plant becomes older it produces offsets which enhance its appearance. The Old Lady Cactus is free-flowering in the spring and summer, producing the characteristic halo of flowers, in this case of a beautiful cerise-red, and appearing through the white 'hair' at the top of the plant.

Mammillaria zeilmanniana

If only one mammillaria is to be selected for the collection, *M. zeilmanniana*, commonly called the Rose Pin-cushion, is probably the one to grow. The plant produces a wealth of bright pinkish-purple flowers from an early age, during the summer. These flowers are a little larger than the norm for mammillaria, measuring up to 19mm (¾in) across. But watch out for the hooked spines which stand out from the fine bristles covering the plant.

The free-flowering *Mammillaria zeilmanniana.*

Notocactus haselbergii

The notocactus are all commonly called Ball Cacti and originate from South America. Although relatively slow-growing, *N. haselbergii* can produce a stem measuring up to 12.5cm (5in) across. The small, soft spines give the plant an attractive, silvery appearance.

Notocactus tend not to flower well when small, but the blooms are worth waiting for. *N. haselbergii* produces beautiful orange-red flowers at the top of the plant although they are smaller in size than some other Notocactus.

Notocactus scopa

This plant always looks attractive, even from being a small, young plant. Apart from producing fine white spines, it also has slightly larger red-brown spines, contrasting superbly and providing a most effective pattern.

In time, *N. scopa* can grow to approximately 10cm (4in) in height and produces magnificent bright yellow flowers that can measure about 5cm (2in) across.

Opuntia microdasys var. albispina

The *Opuntia* family is the largest genus of cacti, with approximately 300 species. Although many of these are rather large, even awkward, a number of varieties are good for collections.

Opuntias are often commonly called Prickly Pears, due to the pear-shaped fruit produced by *O. cochinelifera*.

O. microdasys var. *albispina* is a very attractive form without spines, but having spots of white glochids or bristles. Take care when handling the plant as the glochids have hooks on the end that can catch all too easily in your fingers. Although it

Notocactus scopa in flower.

Notocactus scopa, very spiny.

very rarely flowers, if conditions are good the plant will produce light yellow flowers.

Opuntia microdasys var. rufida

Similar to *O. microdasys* var. *albispina*, this species produces relatively small pads that are compact and are covered with reddish-brown glochids. The compact form of the plant displays the pads well, unlike many opuntias which grow lank and straggly. The hooked bristles of glochids should again be avoided, even though they may look quite harmless to the unwary.

Unfortunately, the plant rarely flowers – but if it does, it produces yellow flowers. Both varieties of *O. microdasys* are sometimes called by the common name, Bunny Ears.

Opuntia robusta

One of the taller growing opuntias that may be worth growing in a collection, although fortunately it does not grow as large as it would in its native surroundings, it nevertheless can, in time, grow either too large or somewhat untamed as the relatively large pads grow out of balance with the plant.

Fortunately, the plant is quite tough and can tolerate either strong pruning to remove wayward growth – which may then be suitably prepared for propagation to replace the original plant or alternatively the old plant may be retained. After pruning, the old plant will usually produce fresh growth although the original pads will age and look much less attractive than the new ones.

O. robusta produces yellow flowers in the wild but very rarely flowers in cultivation.

Pachycereus pringlei

Commonly called the Organ Pipe Cactus, this one originates from Mexico. Growing to very large dimensions in its native state, it could reach 10m (33ft) in height, but this should not deter you from including the plant in your collection if it appeals to you.

Similar in some ways to the carnegiea (Giant Saguaro Cactus) the pachycereus as it grows conjures up the feeling of the 'Western' cactus with characteristic heavily-ribbed stems and, as it reaches maturity, columnar branches which add much character to the plant.

Opuntia microdasys var. albispina.

Pachycereus pringlei.

Pachypodium saundersii

This most extraordinary succulent originates from South Africa and Madagascar and has a swollen stem covered with quite vicious spines.

Pachypodiums are normally raised from seed which is contained in fruits which form after the plant has flowered, which in the case of *P. saundersii* are white.

At its tip the pachypodium produces dark green leaves in the spring; these are deciduous and shed by the plant each year.

Apart from *P. saundersii*, there are about eleven other species with flowers of yellow, orange and red as well as white.

Parodia mutabilis

Parodia are generally small, measuring just 7.5cm (3in) in diameter, and they flower in great profusion. Unfortunately, they are more difficult to grow than many other cacti and great care should be taken with watering, otherwise roots may be lost and if this occurs the plant may then die.

However, if their care can be mastered, the rewards are worthwhile. *P. mutabilis* is probably one of the most attractive parodia, producing yellow or orange flowers.

Originating from Argentina, *P. mutabilis* also has hooked spines borne on the globular-shaped body.

Flowering in great profusion, *Parodia mutabilis*.

Yellow-flowered variety of *Rebutia senilis*.

Parodia sanguiniflora
Similar to other parodia, this plant has a globular shape in its early years, becoming slightly more columnar as it matures.

The plant produces beautiful blood-red flowers which give the plant its name, and can measure 2.5–4cm (1–1½in) across. As it grows it can sometimes produce offsets which inhibit the lowering of the parent. If this occurs, remove the offsets and pot them singly to start new plants with a better potential for flowering.

Care is again required with watering, but once experience of keeping other cacti and succulents is gained parodia are worth adding to your collection.

Rebutia fiebrigii
Despite their somewhat diminutive size, rebutias are quite extravagant in their amazing display of brilliant-coloured flowers. Unlike many other cacti, the striking flowers – trumpets of orange, red, yellow or white – encircle the stem at a low position, even at its base.

R. fiebrigii measures up to 5cm (2in) in diameter with white spines that are darker at their tips. The numerous, vivid orange flowers will last for several days and as they fade their place is quickly filled by successive flowers.

Rebutia senilis
Commonly called the Fire Crown Cactus, *R. senilis* is another popular and excellent species. The brilliant, fiery-red flowers contrast beautifully with the soft white spines. Typical of all rebutias, the flowers are produced in a long succession in the spring and will last even longer if the plant is lightly shaded from direct, hot sunlight.

Ideally propagated from seed, rebutias are very easy to raise and make good window-sill cacti, where they can be cultivated with very little effort on your part.

Rhipsalidopsis rosea

The very popular Easter Cactus is well known for the extraordinary delicate and elongated pink flowers produced in the spring. It is rather strange in appearance, consisting of flat pads with fluffy, inoffensive spines at the ends.

R. rosea can readily be propagated by lightly inserting the pads in compost, especially as they can easily be removed from the plant. As an epiphyte, or tree-living cactus, in its natural habitat the Easter Cactus prefers to be grown in a compost with a higher humus content and is especially happy if grown in a hanging basket from which the flowers can cascade.

Rhipsalis schaferi

Occasionally called Mistletoe Cacti, rhipsalis can sometimes become straggly and untidy. However, when grown in a hanging basket they make an interesting display.

Surprisingly, this is one of the relatively few cacti that is not only found in America but also Sri Lanka and Africa. Growing as an epiphyte, or tree-living cactus, it prefers less sunlight and more shade than many other cacti and also requires a higher level of humidity. The very attractive flowers range from red to pink and white. R. schaferi is an interesting species with beautiful white flowers, produced on almost cylindrical trailing stems.

Sansevieria trifasciata 'Laurentii'

Much better known as Mother-in-Law's Tongue, this is a very popular and hardy succulent.

The cream-bordered leaves complement the subtle green pattern on the middle of the leaves which can grow to about 75cm (2½ft) tall. Surprisingly, the plant produces a flower spike of many greenish-white

Rhipsalidopsis rosea.

flowers with a delicate sweet scent, provided they are cared for correctly and not over-watered.

The pot will in time become filled with the offsets produced by the plant and these exert so much pressure on the pot that it will often split if it is of plastic or fracture if it is a clay pot.

The offsets may be carefully removed by severing the joining stem with a sharp knife and then gently teasing the roots apart. Offsets should be about half of the height of the parent plant before being removed and potted. Do not propagate S. trifasciata 'Laurentii' from leaf cuttings, i.e. by cutting the leaves into sections to propagate, otherwise the cream and green variegation will be lost and the resultant plant will revert to being all green.

Sansevieria hahnii

This more diminutive form of sansevieria, compared to the Mother-in-Law's Tongue, is a more compact plant which shares the benefits of being easy to grow, although not anywhere near as colourful – lacking the cream edge to the leaves. These are also carried in a less erect fashion, resembling an informal rosette when viewed from above.

Commonly called the Bird's Nest Sansevieria, *S. hahnii* should be treated in the same way as all sansevierias with regard to watering. Being succulents, they do not like being kept too moist, preferring rather to be grown on the dry side. If not, rotting is very likely to occur, and there will be little chance of saving the plant.

Schlumbergera

This cactus is very popular at Christmas and during the winter, when it provides a feast of colour during the drab grey days when little else is in flower. Most commonly called the Christmas Cactus, its very showy flowers are produced on the ends of the flattish pads. The flowers are usually pink or purple and are complex in shape, the petals peeling back along the length of the elongated flowers.

Being another epiphytic cactus that grows on branches up in the trees in the rain forest jungles of South America, the plant prefers a higher level of moisture and humidity. Take care to avoid temperature fluctuations when it is in bud, otherwise rapid bud drop may result.

Scilla violacea

This quite unusual succulent adds a touch of unusual interest to a collection. Commonly called the Silver Squill, it produces a bulb at the base, which grows partly above and partly below the surface of the soil. The light- to mid-green leaves are prettily patterned with dark green markings. As the plant grows, further bulbous offsets are produced which may be separated from the parent plant and propagated.

Dainty blue flowers appear on erect stems in the spring, once the plant reaches maturity – but this will not be for several years.

Scilla violacea.

Variegated *Sansevieria hahnii*.

45

Red-tinged *Sedum rubrotinctum*.

Sedum rubrotinctum

Sedums are very popular succulent plants with many varieties that are even grown as hardy garden plants. The habit of sedums is generally trailing, although some species such as *S. spectabile* are more erect, producing attractive heads of many small flowers on a single stem that often attract butterflies and bees.

Sometimes called Christmas Cheer, *S. rubrotinctum* has succulent, oval, mid-green leaves with a beautiful red tinge at the tips. Yellow flowers appear on the ends of the stems, usually in the spring.

Selenicereus grandiflorus

Selenicereus or Moon Cactus is really only worth growing in a greenhouse collection because it has a rather straggly and rampant habit of growth.

Probably the most attractive and romantic species is *S. grandiflorus* or Queen of the Night. Flowers that measure 20–30cm (8–12in) across and are sweetly scented are produced during the night but fade by

Bead-like *Senecio rowleyanus*.

morning. Growing to 1.5–4m (5–13ft), the plant requires the support of canes or some other structure to hold the plant securely. It also needs a temperature of around 20–21°C (60–70°F) and moderate to high humidity.

Senecio rowleyanus

Occasionally called *Kleinia rowleyanus*, this unusual succulent is aptly commonly named String of Beads because of the way its bead-like leaves cascade in strings. Although a rather loose and straggly plant, it is quite novel, as indeed are many of the kleinia. It is best grown as a trailing plant in a hanging basket, producing small white flowers. The delicate trails of *K. rowleyanus* can measure up to 45–60cm (1½-2ft) long.

Stapelia hirsuta

Stapelia are also called Starfish Flowers, which is certainly a great deal more pleasant than its other name of Carrion Flower.

The fleshy, angular stems are only moderately interesting but the flowers are most extraordinary, many species producing bold flowers of an interesting pattern and often with the strong smell, even stench, of carrion or rotting meat which attracts flies to pollinate them.

S. hirsuta has a less pungent smell and produces magnificent reddish-brown flowers with a mauve hairy covering. The flowers, measuring up to 7.5–10cm (3–4in) in diameter, are among the most unusual produced by succulents.

Stapelia variegata

Also known as the Toad Cactus and probably the most popular of the stapelias, this plant has fleshy, angular, grey-green stems and grows to only 10–15cm (4–6in) in height. However, the flowers are rather special. Measuring approximately 6.5cm (2½in) in diameter, these yellow, five-petalled flowers with reddish-brown flecks and lines can be off-putting and may require you to banish them to the greenhouse where they will do no harm!

Trichocereus chilensis

These very long-lived cacti do not grow to a large size in normal cultivation; indeed, they may only attain 25cm (10in) after a considerable time. The plant produces quite vicious buff-coloured spines that are usually distinctly darker at the tip.

T. chilensis is very suitable for a collection where shortage of space is a problem, as the plant is both slow growing and of moderate proportions. If you are lucky enough to obtain a mature specimen, or alternatively keep the plant for a number of years, you will be rewarded by white flowers up to 12.5cm (5in) in length and having a superb scent.

Stapelia variegata, toad cactus.

Flower of Stapelia variegata.

47

INDEX AND ACKNOWLEDGEMENTS

Picture credits

Pat Brindley: 1,4/5,9(t),10,14(r),15(t),26/7,30(b),31,33(b),
    36(r),37(b),38(b),39(b),40(b),41(l),45(b),46(r).
Ron & Christine Foord: 9(b),19,22(t,b),23(t,b),30(t),32,
    34(bl),35(r),36(l),38(t),39(l),40(t),42,45(t).
John Hayward: 11,12,14(l).
Harry Smith Horticultural Photographic Collection: 6,7,8,9(c),
    15(b),18,28(bl,br),29(t,b),33(t),34(br),35(l),37(t),41(r),
    43,44,46(l),47(l,r).

Artwork by Simon Roulstone